The Little Pink Book Of Cancer Cartoons

Kate Matthews

Text and Art © 2011 by Kate Matthews

All rights reserved under the Pan-American and the International Copyright conventions.

This book may not be reproduced in whole or in part, in any form, or by any means, mechanical or electronic, including photocopying, recording, scanning or by any information storage and retrieval system now known or hereafter invented, without written permission from the author.

ISBN 978-1-105-24360-8

First Printing

Introduction:

In July of 2010, I found a lump in my right breast. The findings got even scarier when doctors discovered a second tumor in my other breast. I had always been rather ambidextrous, but this was ridiculous!

Many of the books I read advised me to keep a journal to help sort through my feelings. I dutifully followed this advice, but the words I penned were so darkly poisonous it seemed they might be able to cause cancer all by themselves. I had to find a different way to cope, so I started looking for any little bit of humor I could find.

Though I've often had ideas for cartoons, I never drew any of them for the simple reason that my freehand drawing skills suck. This has stopped me from many an artistic endeavor in the past, but with death maybe looming, I finally gave myself permission to draw anyway. That's one of cancer's little gifts: you discover that it's OK to do the things that matter to you, despite what others might think.

These little cartoons helped me to cope with the fear and the absurdity of having a life-threatening disease. Though cancer humor can be grim, I'm convinced that even ironic laughter is healthier than terror or rage. I offer this book to the many men and women are traveling through breast cancer's corridors.

Dedication

Special thanks to my wonderful husband, children and my sister Elizabeth, who stood by me through the darkest days, and to my good friend Claire Mills, the fantastic doctors at Stanford, my amazing surgeon Dr. Gordon Lee and to a great oncologist: Dr. Robert D'Acquisto.

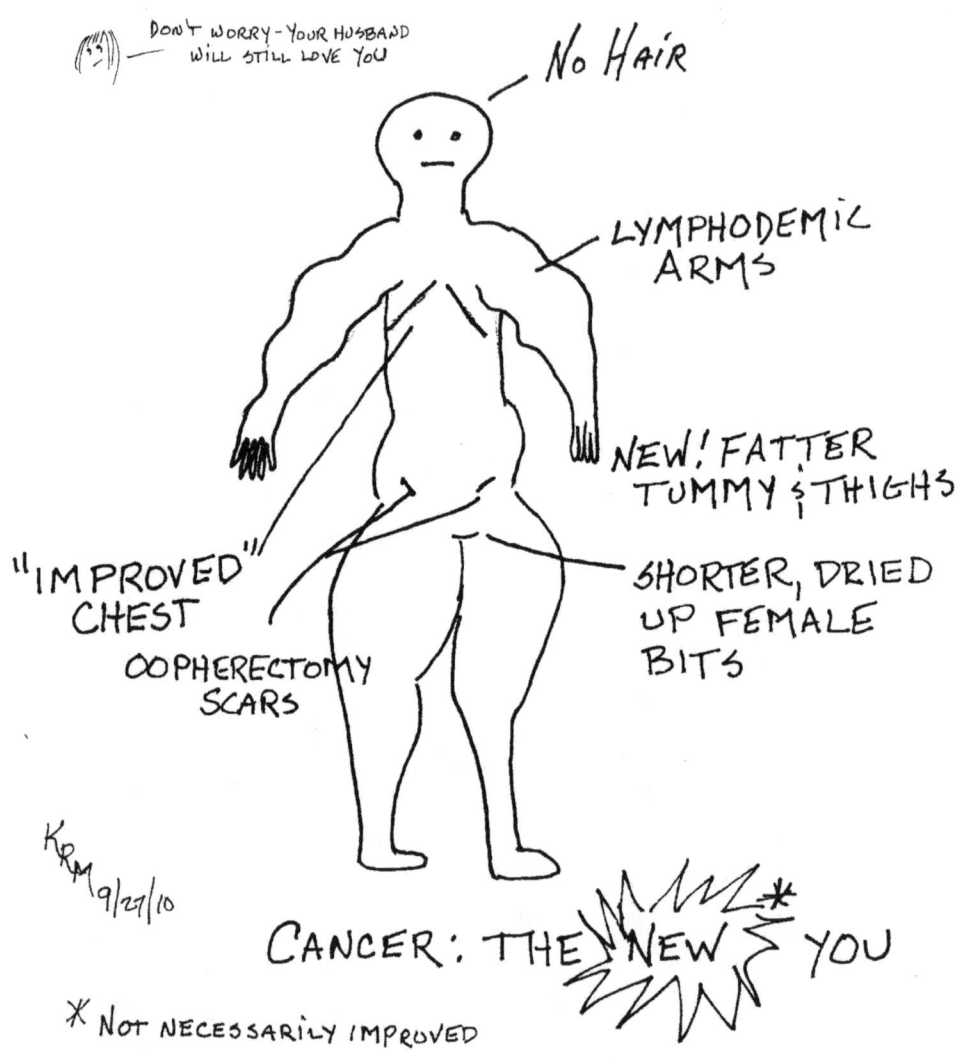

?!? / WHERE ARE THOSE KEYS?

KEYS

NEWSFLASH!

CHEMOBRAIN STARTS <u>BEFORE</u> THEY START CHEMO

KRM 9/22/10

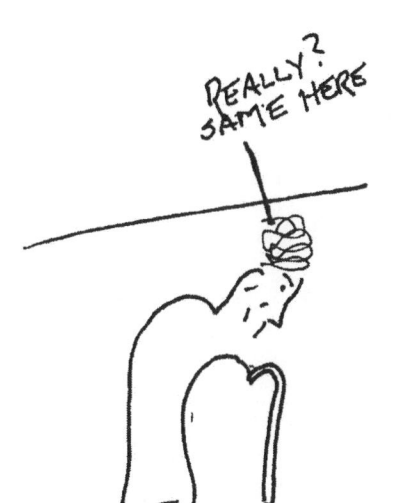

Feminist Rally

Sign: BREASTS & HOW THEY IMPRISON US

IF OUR BREASTS ARE THAT USELESS, WHY DON'T THEY JUST DRY UP & FALL OFF AFTER 50?

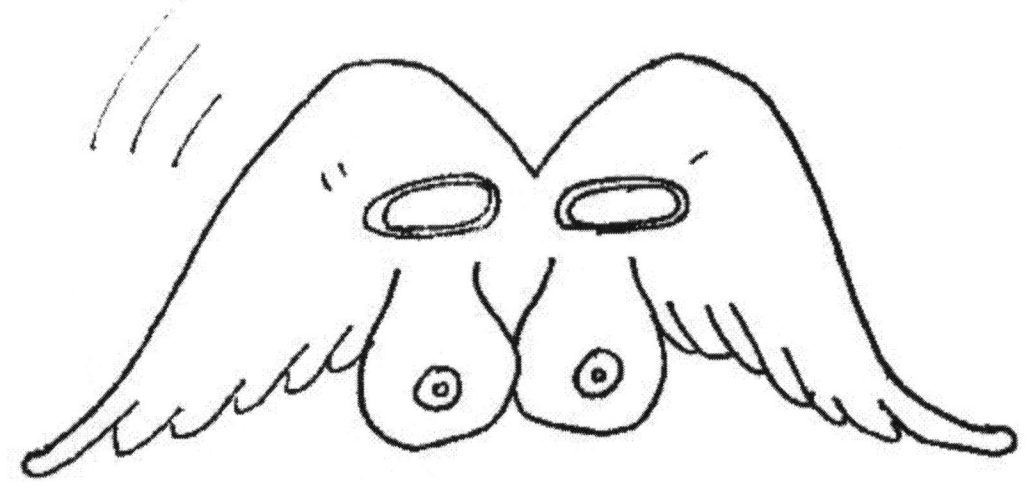

Boob Heaven

KRM
9/29/10

SHE MIGHT HAVE NEW FOOBS
BUT IT'S STILL THE SAME OLD
MARTA!

KRM 9/15/10

KRM 9/20/10

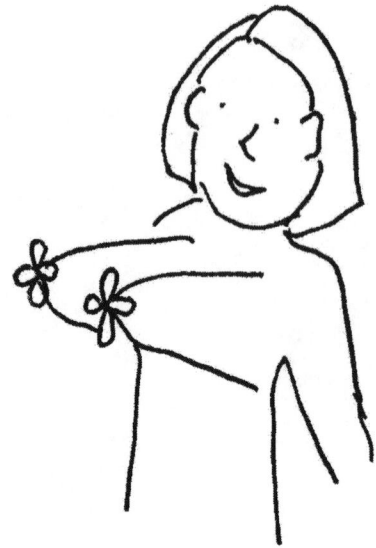

THE DAY BEFORE MY MASTECTOMY

HAVE MY HUSBAND COME IN.
HE'D BE HAPPY TO HELP
WITH THE "VIGOROUS" BREAST
MASSAGE

KRM
11/26/10

LYMPHO GRAPHIA

Why yes, I would appreciate a little help with my baggage

NUCLEAR MEDICINE DEPT

"Now don't be alarmed if you see a little glow after you turn the lights off"

KRM 10/26/10

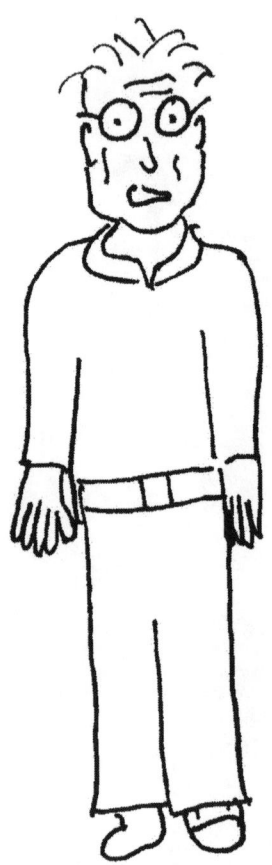

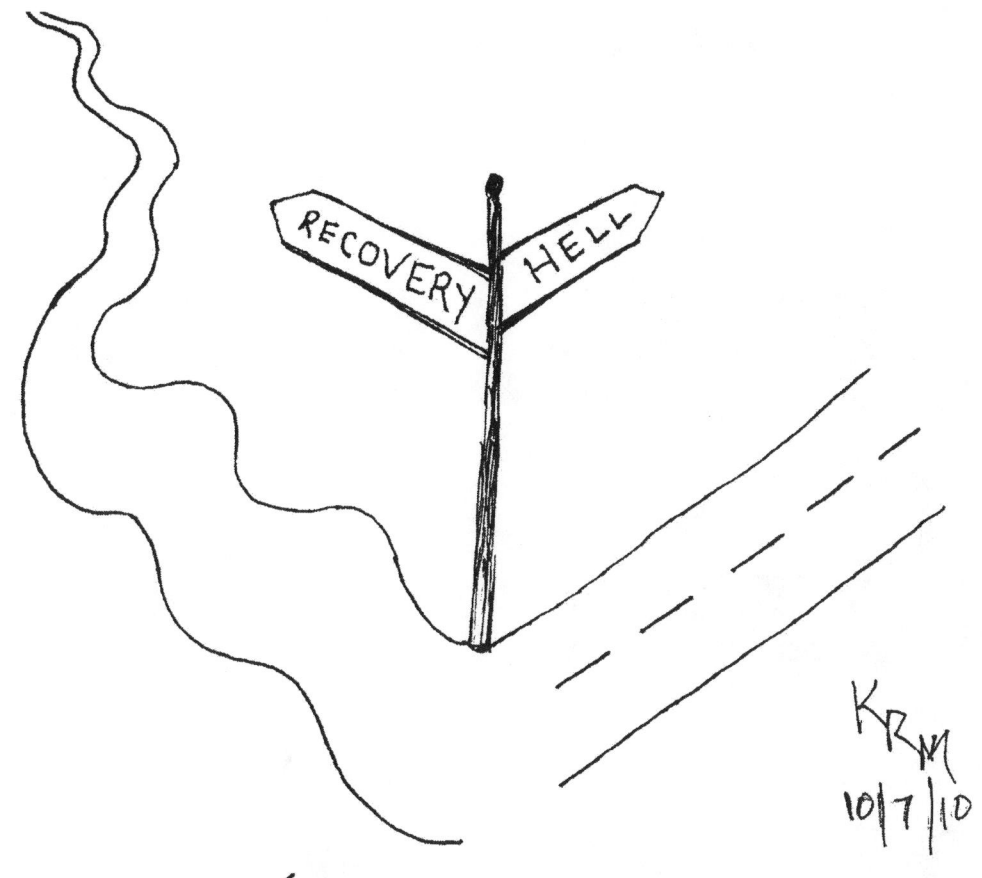

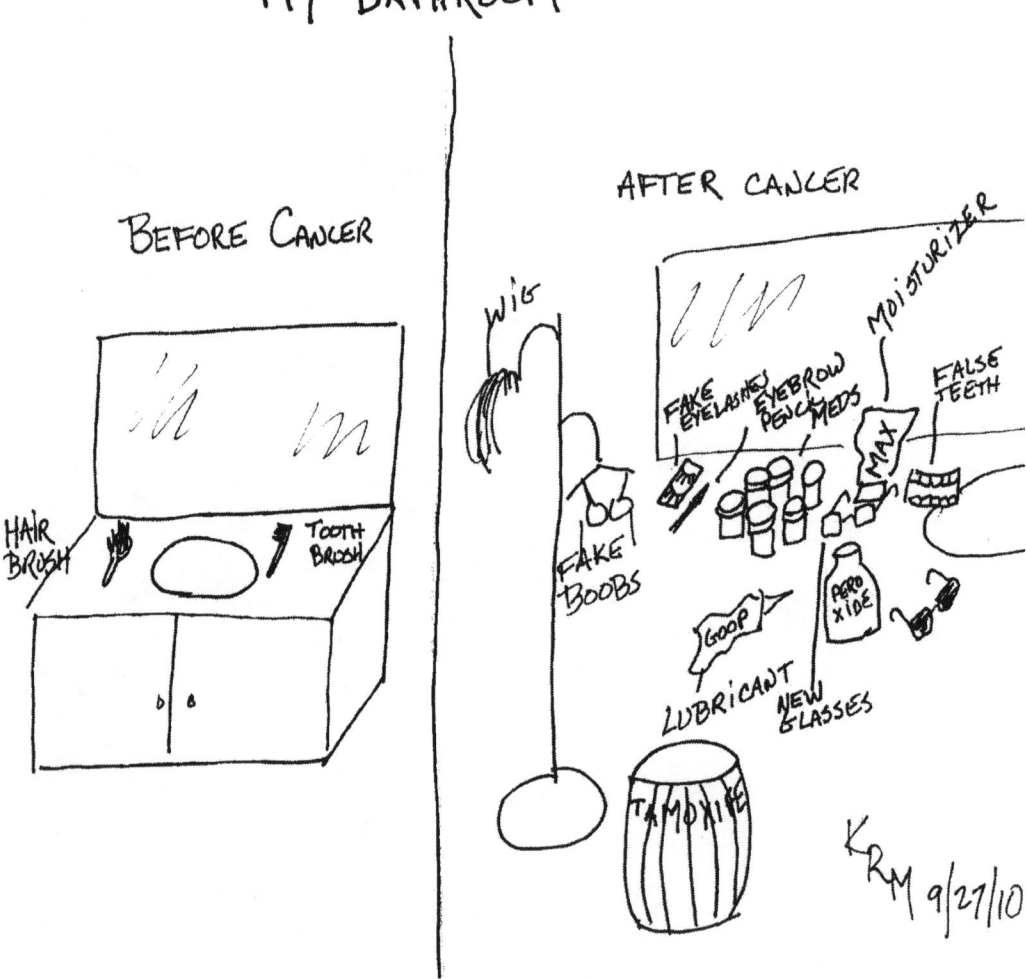

After her DIEP surgery

Too bad they didn't also fix my butt!

KRM
9/24/10

Silly Thought #1

 I'M LOOKING FORWARD TO CHEMO — IT'LL BE JUST LIKE A LITTLE VACATION!

KRM
1/31/11

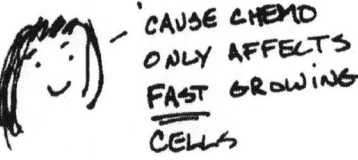

I JUST PUKED UP MY ANTI-NAUSEA PILL.

KRM
2/8/11

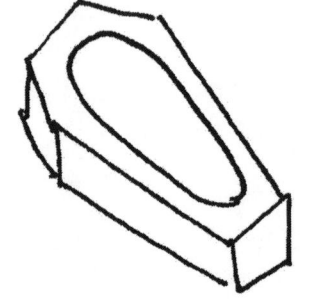

IT'S STARTING TO LOOK COZIER

KRM 9/27/10

Wow! The timing for this couldn't be better!

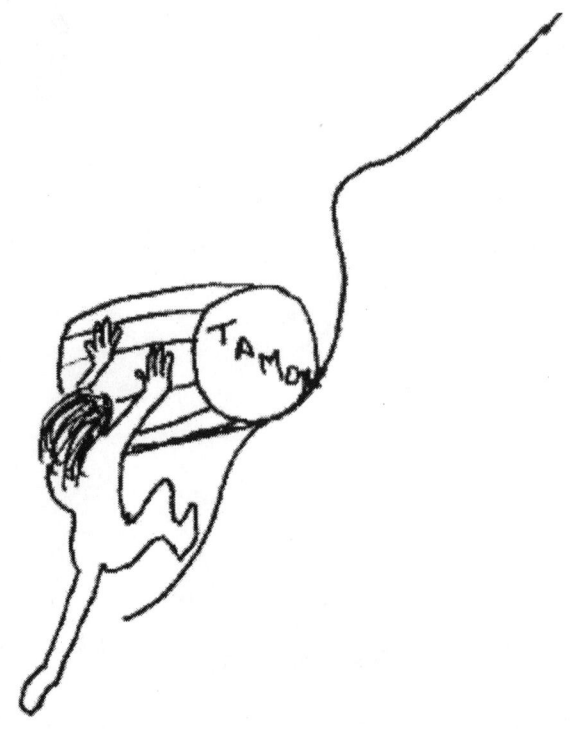

My hair is finally growing back. Now people think I'm a lesbian

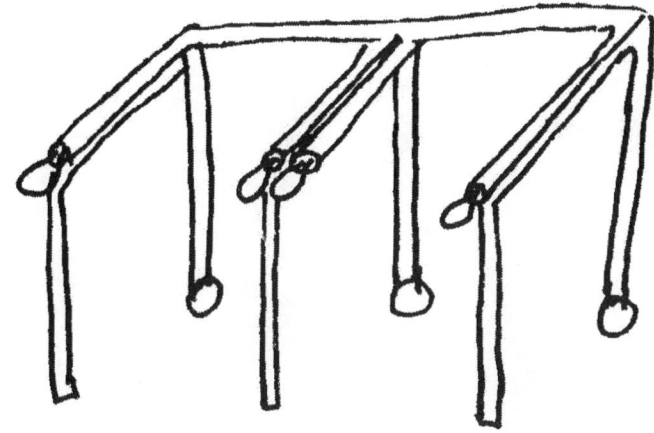

Made in the USA
Lexington, KY
01 April 2012